New Orleans
PELICANS

BY K.C. KELLEY

Published by The Child's World®
1980 Lookout Drive • Mankato, MN 56003-1705
800-599-READ • www.childsworld.com

Cover: © Jim Mone/AP Images.
Photographs ©: AP Images: 9; Ann Heisenfelt 17; Butch Dill 21;
Christopher Record 29. Dreamstime.com: Maomatou 13. Imagn/USA
Today Sports: Nelson Chenault 6; Derek Hingle 26; Tim Fuller 26;
Justin Ford 26. Newscom: Brian Rothmuller/Icon SW 5, 26; Stephen Lew/
Icon SW 12, 25; Pedro Portal/MCT 18; George Bridges/MCT 22.

ISBN 9781503824683
LCCN 2018964286

Printed in the United States of America
PA02416

ABOUT THE AUTHOR

K.C. Kelley is a huge sports fan who has
written more than 150 books for kids.
He has written about football, basketball,
soccer, and even auto racing! He lives in
Santa Barbara, California.

TABLE OF
CONTENTS

GO, PELICANS!

When does a hornet turn into a pelican? The answer is, "When an NBA team changes its name!" The New Orleans Hornets became the Pelicans in 2013. The team chose the new name after the state bird of Louisiana. Like the bird, the NBA Pelicans hope to fly high. Pelicans fans hope for an NBA championship! Let's meet the Pelicans!

Jahlil Okafor of the Pelicans waits for a rebound in a game against the Los Angeles Clippers.

5

Jrue Holiday leads the Pelicans against the Grizzlies. NOLA on his jersey is a nickname for New Orleans.

WHO ARE THE PELICANS?

The Pelicans are one of 30 NBA teams. The Pelicans play in the Southwest Division of the Western Conference. The other Southwest Division teams are the Dallas Mavericks, the Houston Rockets, the Memphis Grizzlies, and the San Antonio Spurs. The Pelicans have tough battles with their Southwest Division **rivals**.

WHERE THEY CAME FROM

The NBA added the New Orleans Hornets as a new team in 2002. In 2005, the team and the city faced a bad storm. **Hurricane** Katrina crashed into the New Orleans area. The team's home arena was damaged. The Hornets had to play two seasons in Oklahoma City. In 2007, they moved back and had one of their best seasons ever! The storm united the city and the team.

Fans in Oklahoma City welcomed the team after Hurricane Katrina forced a short-term move.

Anthony Davis was the team's biggest star until he left in 2019.

WHO THEY PLAY

The Pelicans play 82 games each season. They play 41 games at home and 41 on the road. The Pelicans play four games against each of the other Southwest Division teams. They play 36 games against other Western Conference teams. The Pelicans also play each of the teams in the Eastern Conference twice. That's a lot of basketball! Each June, the winners of the Western and Eastern Conferences play each other in the NBA Finals.

WHERE THEY PLAY

The Smoothie King Center in New Orleans is home to more than just the Pelicans. Local fans have watched hockey, indoor football, and pro wrestling inside the huge building. Gymnastics and volleyball events have also been held in the arena, which opened in 2002. During Pelicans games, fans get help from the team **mascot**. Pierre the Pelican dances and helps fans cheer for their favorite team!

The Smoothie King Center stands in front of a New Orleans sunset. At Pelicans games, Pierre the Pelican helps fans cheer (left).

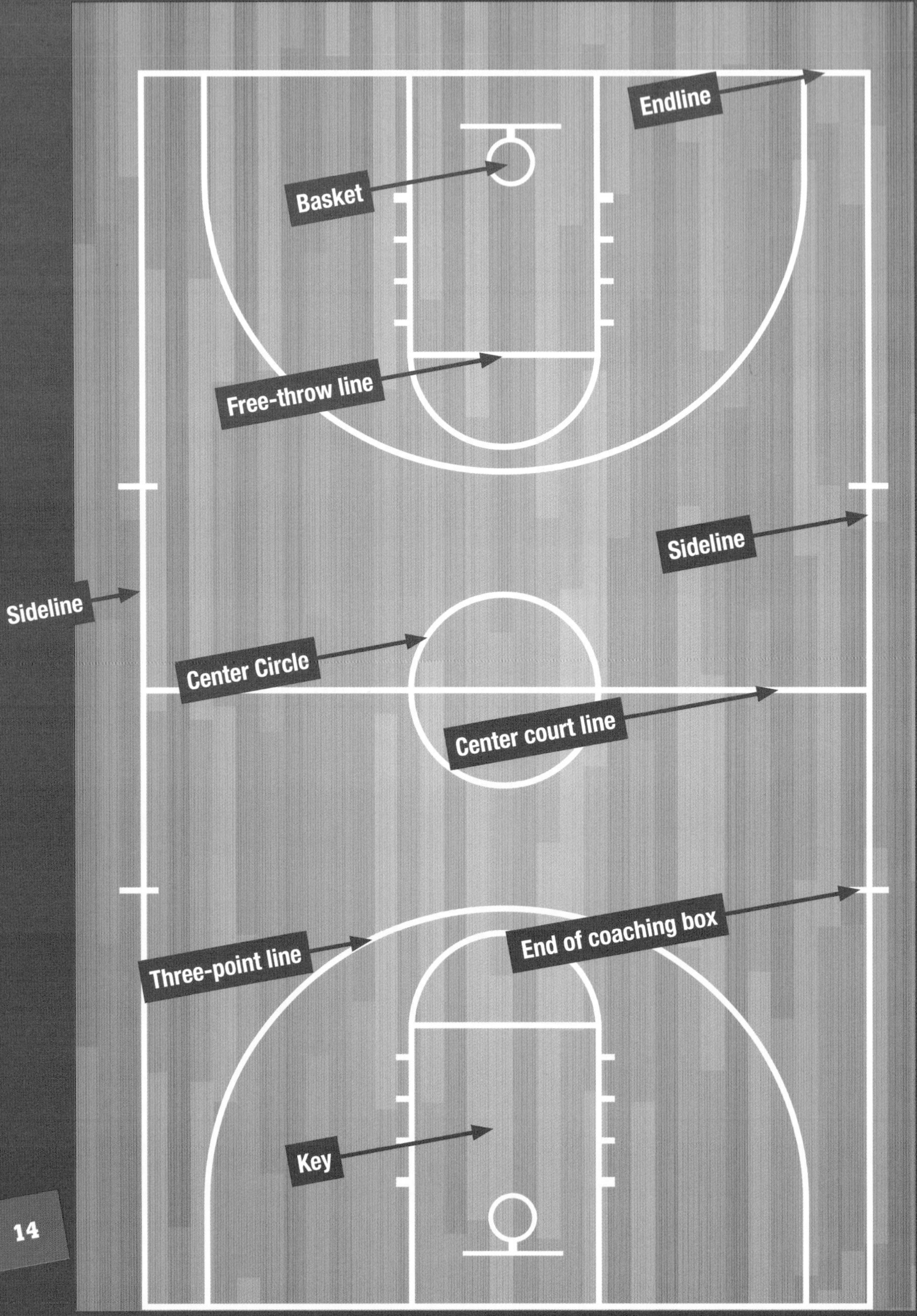

Endline

Basket

Free-throw line

Sideline

Sideline

Center Circle

Center court line

Three-point line

End of coaching box

Key

THE BASKETBALL COURT

An NBA court is 94 feet long and 50 feet wide (28.6 m by 15.24 m). Nearly all the courts are made from hard maple wood. Rubber mats under the wood help make the floor springy. Each team paints the court with its **logo** and colors. Lines on the court show the players where to take shots. The diagram on the left shows the important parts of the NBA court.

How can you have a rain delay in an indoor arena? The Pelicans had one in 2018. A leak in the roof during a storm let water onto the court. The game was stopped while workers mopped up the water!

GOOD TIMES

Most new NBA teams struggle to win. The Pelicans, though, got off to a good start. The team made the NBA **playoffs** in each of its first two seasons. The Pelicans' best season ever came in 2007–08. They set a team record with 56 wins. They won their first Southwest Division championship, too.

David West rises up for a shot in the 2008 playoffs. New Orleans did very well that season.

Three against one! Al-Farouq Aminu tried to score in 2012. The Pelicans struggled like this all season.

TOUGH TIMES

The Pelicans have had more losing seasons than winning seasons. Their lowest point came in 2004–05. They lost a team-record 64 games that season. From 2011 through 2016, they finished last in the Southwest Division each year. With superstar Anthony Davis leaving in 2019, the Pelicans might have some struggles ahead, too.

ALL THE RIGHT MOVES

Most NBA players are very good in one area. They might be a great shooter. They could be good at defense. A player who is very good at both is rare. Jrue Holiday of the Pelicans is one of those special players. He leads the team with great passes and good shooting. He is also one of the top defensive players in the NBA. He's a double threat!

Tough D! Jrue Holiday stays between this Rockets player and the basket.

David West was a two-time All-Star during his eight seasons with New Orleans.

HEROES THEN

The first star for the Pelicans was sharp-shooting forward P.J. Brown. He helped the Pelicans reach the playoffs in their first two seasons. Guard Chris Paul began his great career with six Pelicans seasons. Paul is a terrific **ball handler**. He led the NBA in **assists** and **steals** twice each. David West was a two-time All-Star with New Orleans. He is still second all-time in points among Pelicans players.

HEROES NOW

Veteran guard Jrue Holiday piles in points for the Pelicans. Holiday is one of three brothers who all play in the NBA! As a guard, Holiday passes the ball to teammates such as E'Twaun Moore so they can score. Forward Julius Randle is a top **rebounder**. Darius Miller, another forward, helps with a great shooting touch.

Julius Randle rises above the floor—and the opposing team—to drop in two points for the Pelicans.

WHAT THEY WEAR

NBA players wear a **tank top** jersey. Players wear team shorts. Each player can choose his own sneakers. Some players also wear knee pads or wrist guards.

Each NBA team has more than one jersey style. The pictures at left show some of the Pelicans' jerseys.

The NBA basketball is 29.5 inches (75 cm) around. It is covered with leather. The leather has small bumps called pebbles.

The pebbles on a basketball help players grip it.

TEAM STATS

Here are some of the all-time career records for the New Orleans Pelicans. These stats are complete through all of the 2018–19 NBA regular season.

GAMES

David West	530
Anthony Davis	466

POINTS PER GAME

Anthony Davis	23.7
Jamal Mashburn	21.5

THREE-POINTERS

Peja Stojakovic	553
Ryan Anderson	533

REBOUNDS PER GAME

Tyson Chandler	11.3
Anthony Davis	10.5

STEALS PER GAME

Chris Paul	2.4
Baron Davis	2.1

FREE-THROW PCT.

Peja Stojakovic	,893
Ryan Anderson	.868

CHRIS PAUL

29

ASSISTS PER GAME

Chris Paul	9.9
Greivis Vasquez	7.4

GLOSSARY

assists *(uh-SISTS)* passes that lead directly to a basket

ball handler *(BAWL HAND-ler)* in basketball, a player who is skilled at dribbling and passing

forward *(FORE-word)* a player in basketball who usually plays away from the basket

guard *(GARD)* a player in basketball who dribbles and makes passes

hurricane *(HER-ih-kane)* a swirling, wind-driven storm that moves from the ocean to land

mascot *(MASS-kot)* a costumed character who helps fans cheer

playoffs *(PLAY-offs)* games played between top teams to determine who moves ahead

rebounder *(REE-bownd-er)* a player who catches missed shots

rivals *(RYE-vuhlz)* two people or groups competing for the same thing

tank top *(TANK TOP)* a style of shirt that has straps over the shoulders and no sleeves

veteran *(VET-uh-run)* an athlete who has played several pro seasons

FIND OUT MORE

IN THE LIBRARY

Democker, Michael. *Anthony Davis.* Kennett
Square, PA: Purple Toad, 2017.

Sports Illustrated Kids (editors). *Big Book of Who:
Basketball.* New York: Sports Illustrated Kids, 2015.

Whiting, Jim. *NBA: History of Hoops: New Orleans
Pelicans.* Mankato, MN: Creative Paperbacks, 2017.

ON THE WEB

Visit our website for links about the New Orleans Pelicans:
childsworld.com/links

Note to Parents, Teachers, and Librarians: We routinely verify our Web links to make sure
they are safe and active sites. So encourage your readers to check them out!

INDEX